Mercury, Venus, Earth, and Mars

By Gregory Vogt

Raintree Steck-Vaughn Publishers

A Harcourt Company

Austin · New York

www.steck-vaughn.com

OUR UNIVERSE

Published by Raintree Steck-Vaughn Publishers,
an imprint of Steck-Vaughn Company.

Library of Congress Cataloging-in-Publication Data
Vogt, Gregory.
    Mercury, Venus, Earth, and Mars/by Gregory Vogt.
       p.cm. (Our universe)
    Includes index.
    ISBN 0-7398-3110-0
    1. Mercury (Planet)--Juvenile literature. 2. Venus (Planet)--Juvenile literature.
3. Earth--Juvenile literature. 4. Mars (Planet)--Juvenile literature. I. Title.
QB606 .V64 2000

                                   00-058772

Printed in the United States of America
10 9 8 7 6 5 4 3 2 1 W 02 01 00

Produced by Compass Books

Photo Acknowledgments
Digital Stock, 32; All photographs courtesy of NASA.

Content Consultant
David Jewitt
Professor of Astronomy
University of Hawaii Institute for Astronomy

Contents

Diagram of the Inner Planets

Mercury

Rocky mantle   Iron core

Venus

Mantle   Core

Earth

Mars

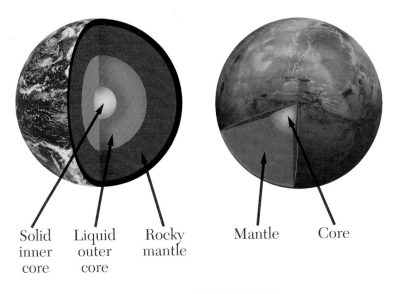

Solid inner core   Liquid outer core   Rocky mantle

Mantle   Core

A Quick Look at the Inner Planets

What is a planet?
A planet is a large ball of gas or rock that circles a star.

How many planets are there?
There are nine known planets in our solar system. The planets circle a star called the Sun. Scientists believe there are more planets that circle other stars.

What are the terrestrial planets?
The terrestrial planets are the four planets closest to the Sun. These inner planets are made mostly of rock.

What is the largest terrestrial planet?
Earth is the largest terrestrial planet.

Which of the terrestrial planets have moons?
Earth and Mars have moons. Earth has one moon, and Mars has two moons. Mercury and Venus have no moons.

Planets in the Solar System

Long ago, ancient peoples saw that stars moved in certain paths through the sky. But they also saw round-shaped objects that moved differently than stars. People named these objects "planets" because of the way they moved. The word "planet" comes from the Greek word for wanderer.

Planets are part of our solar system. The solar system is the Sun and all the objects that circle it. The Sun is a star. It is a large ball of very hot gas that gives off heat and light.

There are nine known planets in our solar system. They travel around the Sun in paths called orbits. Some planets are close to the Sun, and others are very far away from it. Some of the planets have moons that travel around them.

How the Solar System Formed

Most scientists believe our solar system formed many millions of years ago in a nebula. A nebula is a giant cloud of gas and dust. Most nebulas contain a great deal of hydrogen gas. One idea is that a shock wave from an exploding star crashed into the nebula. This powerful wave of energy made the nebula collapse into a flat disk. The disk began to spin. The gas and dust were pulled together by gravity. Gravity is a natural force that attracts objects to each other.

Most of the gas and dust fell to the center of the nebula and became the Sun. The gas got very hot. The hydrogen gas began to turn into helium. Energy from this process was released as light and heat.

Leftover gas and dust formed smaller clumps. The gravity of the Sun pulled on these clumps. They began to orbit the Sun. Smaller clumps joined together when they crashed into each other. They became larger clumps. The clumps continued to grow over millions of years until they became planets.

The closest planets to the Sun are made of the heaviest materials. The closest planet to the Sun is Mercury. Venus, Earth, and Mars are next. Each of these planets is made mostly of rock. These planets are often called the inner planets, or the terrestrial planets. Terrestrial means made of earth or land.

Stars like the Sun are forming in this nebula.

Planets farther from the Sun are made of lighter materials. These include the planets Jupiter, Saturn, Uranus, and Neptune. These giant planets are made mostly of gas. People often call these planets the outer planets, or the gas planets. Pluto is the ninth planet. It is made of rock and ice.

All planets rotate, or spin, around an imaginary line called an axis. The ends of the axis are the north and south poles of a planet.

Planets are very different from stars. Stars give off light. But planets only reflect the light from the star they orbit, such as the Sun.

Mercury is the fastest traveling planet. It was named after the speedy Roman god Mercury.

Mercury, the Closest Planet

Mercury is the closest planet to the Sun. It orbits the Sun at an average distance of 36 million miles (58 million km).

Mercury orbits faster than any other planet. It speeds around the Sun at 107,000 miles (172,200 km) per hour. Early Roman people named the planet after their god Mercury. He was a speedy god who carried messages for the other Roman gods.

Mercury travels around the Sun once every 88 Earth days. A planet's year is the time it takes to travel around the Sun. This makes Mercury's year only 88 Earth days long. But Mercury spins very slowly. It takes 59 Earth days to complete one spin.

Mercury is the second smallest planet. It is 3,031 miles (4,878 km) in diameter. Diameter is the distance through a circle. Only Pluto is smaller.

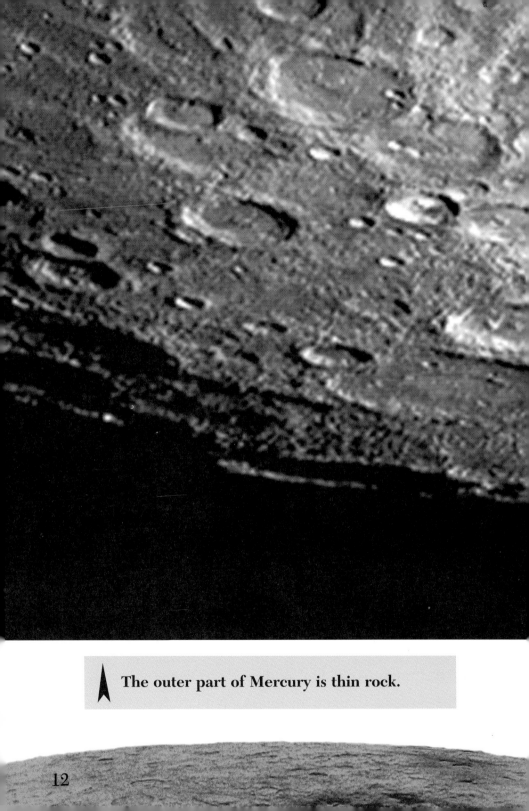

The outer part of Mercury is thin rock.

Seeing Mercury in the Sky

Mercury is the planet closest to the Sun. Because of its position, Mercury is sometimes hidden by the Sun's bright light. That makes Mercury very hard to see from Earth without a telescope. A telescope is a tool that makes faraway objects appear clearer and closer.

When we see it, Mercury looks like a faint star. It always appears close to the horizon. The horizon is the line where the earth and the sky seem to meet.

Mercury's position in the sky changes. Sometimes people can see Mercury in the morning. Mercury seems to rise in the east a few minutes before the Sun.

Parts of Mercury

Mercury has a heavy iron core. A core is the center of something, such as a planet. Mercury's core makes up much of the planet. A layer of molten, or melted, rock surrounds Mercury's iron core. A thin, rocky crust forms the outer surface of the planet.

Mercury's core makes it the second densest planet in the solar system. Density is the amount of matter squeezed into a certain space. Matter is anything that has weight and takes up space. Tightly packed matter in a small area is said to have a high density. Only Earth has a greater density than Mercury.

Mariner 10

U.S. scientists launched the *Mariner 10* space probe on November 3, 1973. A space probe is a craft built to explore and gather information about space. *Mariner 10*'s rocket sent the space probe toward the inner solar system. As it passed by Venus, the planet's gravity changed the direction of *Mariner 10*. The space probe began heading closer to the Sun. A few months later, *Mariner 10* passed by Mercury.

Mariner 10 circled Mercury three times. It took thousands of pictures of the planet. It gathered information about Mercury and sent it back by radio to scientists on Earth.

Mariner 10 ran out of fuel after its third trip around Mercury. It is still orbiting the Sun, but its controls do not work. No other space probe has visited Mercury since *Mariner 10*.

Mercury Today

Scientists learned many things about Mercury from *Mariner 10*. They discovered that Mercury has a very thin atmosphere. An atmosphere is a layer of gases that surrounds a planet. The main gases in Mercury's atmosphere are hydrogen and helium. These gases come from the Sun. The gas surrounds Mercury for a short while before it escapes into space.

A planet's atmosphere acts like a cover to keep heat from immediately escaping into space. This helps keep a planet's surface warm. Mercury has almost no atmosphere. So, it has the widest range of surface temperatures in the whole solar system. During a day on Mercury, the surface changes from very hot to very cold. During the daytime, the temperature reaches about 800° Fahrenheit (427° C). During the nighttime, its temperature drops to –280° Fahrenheit (–138° C).

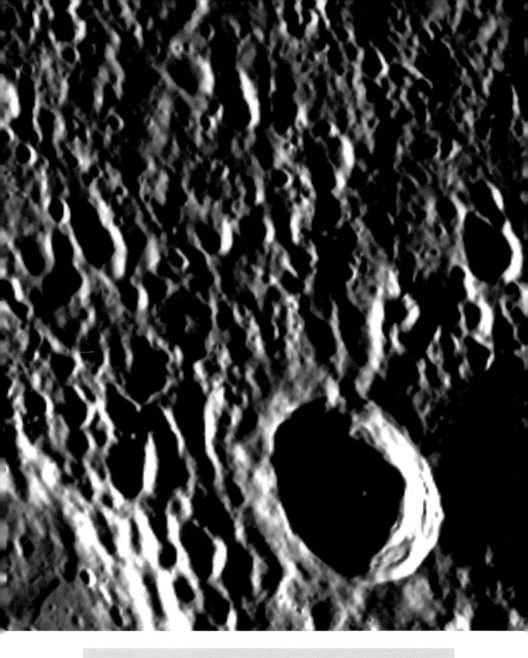

 Mercury's surface is covered with gray rock and many craters.

Mercury's Surface

Mercury has a rocky surface covered with craters. Craters are bowl-shaped holes in the ground. Some large craters have mountains rising from their centers. Meteorites blasted the craters when they smashed into Mercury. Meteorites are rocks that crash into objects in space.

The Caloris Basin is the largest crater on Mercury. It is about 800 miles (1,300 km) across. Large mountains surround the Caloris Basin. Lava has filled much of the Caloris Basin. Lava is liquid rock. Over time, the lava cooled and hardened.

Mercury has other surface features, too. Long, smooth plains stretch between craters. One part of Mercury is covered with hills.

Mercury also has many wrinkles in its surface. Scientists believe the core of the planet was once molten. Mercury shrank when the core cooled and hardened. This made the rock on the planet's surface buckle and wrinkle. The buckling rock formed long cliffs called scarps. These scarps stretch for hundreds of miles.

Astronomers in ancient times named Venus after the Roman god of love and beauty.

Venus, the Cloudy Planet

Venus is nicknamed Earth's twin because it is similar to Earth in some ways. Venus is nearly the same size as Earth. Venus is 7,521 miles (12,104 km) in diameter. Venus and Earth both have thick atmospheres. Venus has very thick clouds that completely surround the planet.

In other ways, Venus is very different from Earth. Venus orbits the Sun at an average distance of 67 million miles (108 million km). It takes Venus 225 Earth days to orbit around the Sun once.

Astronomers discovered that Venus spins in a direction opposite to its orbit. Astronomers are scientists who study objects in space. The direction of its orbit makes Venus spin very slowly. A day on Venus is 243 Earth days long. A day on Venus is longer than its year!

Magellan Mission

Astronomers have sent many space probes to study Venus. A few space probes have tried to land on Venus. One space probe succeeded. The Soviet Union sent the *Venera 13* space probe to Venus in 1982. It landed on Venus and sent information to Earth for 127 minutes before it stopped working.

More than 20 other space probes have orbited the planet. *Magellan* was one space probe that

Radio-Wave Reflections

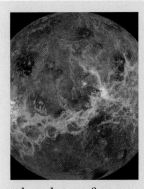

How long the radio waves took to bounce back to *Magellan* told how high the surface was. Waves take longer to bounce back from deep valleys than from high mountains. The strength of the reflections told what the surface was like. Hard, smooth surfaces send back strong reflections. Rough and bumpy surfaces send back weak reflections.

orbited Venus. The United States sent *Magellan* to map the surface of Venus in 1989. It traveled across space and began circling the planet.

The *Magellan* space probe aimed radio waves at Venus. The waves traveled straight through Venus's dense clouds. The waves struck a rough and bumpy surface. They bounced back into space. *Magellan* collected the reflections and sent this information back to Earth by radio. Computers on Earth used the information from *Magellan* to draw maps of the surface of Venus.

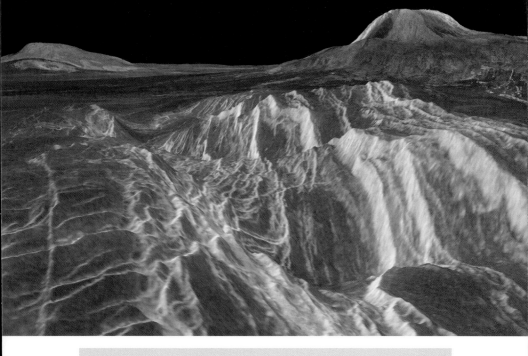

This is a radar picture of volcanoes on Venus's surface.

Surface of Venus

Magellan showed that the surface of Venus was all land with no water oceans. Low-lying plains cover most of its surface. Hardened lava rock covers most of the plains. In some places, its surface is crisscrossed by long cracks and scarps in the rock.

Hills and mountains poke up from parts of Venus's surface. Thousands of volcanoes also dot its surface. Ash, gas, and lava blow out of openings in the tops of these mountains. At 11 miles (17 km) high, the Maxwell Montes volcano is the highest point on Venus. It is two times taller than Mount Everest, the tallest mountain on Earth. Valleys stretch out from some of the volcanoes. Scientists think that flows of fast-moving lava carved these valleys.

Some of the volcanoes on Venus have unusual forms that are different from volcanoes on Earth. From above, some of Venus's volcanoes look like pancakes. They are flat-topped circles about 2,000 feet (610 m) high and 30 to 40 miles (48 to 64 km) across.

Russian scientists named another kind of volcano arachnoid. Arachnoid means spiderlike. These volcanoes are circles that are 30 to 139 miles (50 to 230 km) wide. Cracks stretch out from the circles. The circles look like spider bodies. The cracks look like spiders' legs.

Scientists call another kind of volcano a tick. A tick is a kind of insect. Tick volcanoes have circular shapes and flat tops. Ridges and valleys stretch out from their sides. The ridges and valleys look like a tick's legs.

Venus's clouds make Venus the hottest planet. Its average temperature is about 900° Fahrenheit (482° C).

Effects of Venus's Atmosphere

Venus's atmosphere is made up of poisonous gases. Nitrogen gas makes up 3% of Venus's atmosphere. About 96% of the atmosphere is carbon dioxide. On Earth, people breathe out this gas and breathe in oxygen. Venus has very little oxygen in its atmosphere. People would not be able to breathe on Venus. They would need to bring their own oxygen.

Small water drops make up clouds on Earth. But Venus's clouds are made up of sulfuric-acid fog. This

Through Venus's Atmosphere

A few space probes from Earth have tried to land on Venus. But most space probes have been destroyed on the way down through Venus's atmosphere. Space probes reach the planet's first layer of clouds about 40 miles (64 km) above the surface. There, winds up to 225 miles (362 km) per hour can damage the spacecraft. Space probes then pass through two cloud layers. The air in these layers contains drops of sulfuric acid. Wind storms and lightning rip through the sky and can cause more damage. The air clears at about 31 miles (50 km) above the planet. Winds die down, and it gets warmer.

acid burns skin and melts metal. On Earth, it rains water, but Venus has sulfuric-acid rain.

Venus has a thick atmosphere. It presses down on objects on Venus's surface. This atmospheric pressure is 90 times greater than Earth's atmospheric pressure. The pressure would crush people if they tried to visit Venus.

Venus's carbon dioxide and thick clouds cause the greenhouse effect. Sunlight travels through the atmosphere to Venus's surface. But then the thick clouds act like a blanket. They absorb some heat and reflect it back to the surface instead of letting the heat escape quickly into space.

Earth is nicknamed "the blue planet" because so much of its surface is water.

Earth, the Blue Planet

Earth is the third planet from the Sun. Earth is about 93,000,000 miles (149,668,992 km) away from the Sun. It takes Earth about 365 days to travel around the Sun once. Its orbit is nearly a perfect circle.

Earth is the largest of the inner planets. It is 7,926 miles (12,756 km) in diameter. But it is still small compared to the giant gas planets. About 1,400 planets the size of Earth could fit into one planet the size of Jupiter.

Unlike other planets, Earth's surface is mostly liquid water. Oceans cover 75% of its surface. Islands and large land masses called continents cover the remaining 25% of Earth.

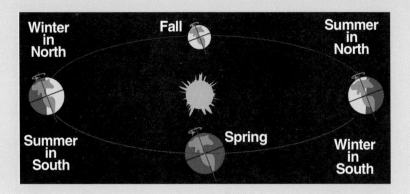

Winter occurs when Earth tilts away from the Sun.

Earth's Axis

While Earth orbits the Sun, it also rotates, or spins, around its axis. The ends of the axis are the North and South Poles. One spin takes about 24 hours. This amount of time is Earth's day.

Earth's axis is tilted 23.5°. For part of its orbit, the North Pole tilts in the Sun's direction. Then it is summer in the northern half of Earth and winter in the southern half of Earth. For part of the year, the South Pole tilts toward the Sun. Then it is summer in the southern half of Earth and winter in the northern half of Earth.

The Atmosphere

Earth's atmosphere is about 78% nitrogen and 21% oxygen. It also contains dust, water vapor, and

Viewing Earth from Space

From a space probe, most of Earth looks blue because of its oceans. The land is green, red, brown, gray, white, and yellow. The colors come from the things on its surface. Deserts are red and yellow. Soil and rock look brown. Ice and snow are white. Swirling white clouds of tiny water drops drift across the blue atmosphere.

very small amounts of other gases. Oxygen is a very important gas for living things. People and animals need oxygen to breathe. Earth's atmosphere also helps control temperatures on the surface. The average temperature for Earth's air is about 60° Fahrenheit (15.5° C).

Earth's atmosphere is made up of several layers. The troposphere is the layer closest to the surface. Most of Earth's air is in the troposphere. Storms and other weather patterns start there.

The stratosphere is above the troposphere. It contains a special kind of oxygen called ozone. Ozone helps protect people from the Sun's harmful rays.

The outer layers are the mesosphere, thermosphere, and exosphere. Most objects from space, such as meteorites, burn up in these layers.

CRUST

Layers of Earth

The core is the center of Earth. The inner core is solid. The outer core is liquid. The mantle is the middle layer of Earth. The crust is the thin, outer layer of Earth.

Parts of Earth

Earth is made up of three parts. The center of the planet is a dense metal and rock core. A layer of heavy rocks called the mantle surrounds the core. Parts of the mantle are molten rock. The crust is the thin, rocky outer layer of the planet.

Earth's crust is divided into giant pieces called plates. Plates move. They slide over molten rock in the mantle.

There are seven continents on Earth. Scientists think the continents were once joined together. They fit together like puzzle pieces. But then they broke apart. Each continent is on a moving plate. Over a long period of time, the plates separated until there were seven large pieces people today call continents.

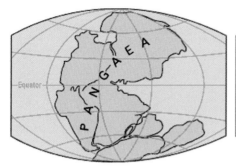

225 million years ago

200 million years ago

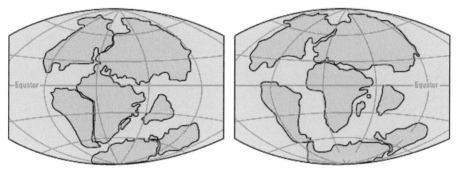

135 million years ago

66 million years ago

PRESENT DAY

This diagram shows how the plates moved apart over millions of years.

Lava flows harden to form black, igneous rock. The rock builds up Earth's surface.

Natural Forces

Natural forces are always changing Earth's crust. The plates and continents move toward or away from each other an inch or two each year. Sometimes plates push against each other. Rock around the plates' edges is forced up and mountains form.

At other times, plate movement causes cracks in the crust called faults. Most faults happen where two plates meet each other. Many volcanoes form and earthquakes happen where these moving plates meet.

On the ocean floor, molten rock from deep inside the mantle oozes to the surface. It flows onto the crust. There it hardens and builds more crust. Lava flows build volcanic mountains.

Water also changes the shape of Earth's land. Rain and wind wear down the volcanoes, mountains, and rock. This process is called erosion. Tiny pieces of rock pile up in low spots and become soil for plants. Earth's surface is always being built up and being worn down.

Earth is not as hot or cold as other planets. It has the right temperature range for water to exist in all its forms. If Earth were as hot as Venus, all the liquid water would turn into water vapor. If Earth were as cold as Mars, all the liquid water would freeze into ice.

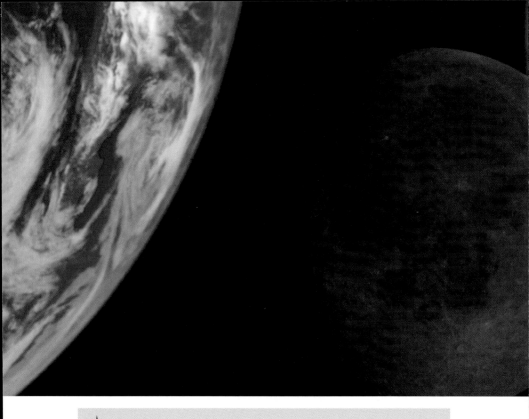

The Moon travels around Earth.

The Moon

Earth has one moon orbiting it. It is called the Moon. The Moon is a rocky ball about 2,160 miles (3,476 km) in diameter. It orbits at an average distance of 238,000 miles (383,024 km) away from Earth. The Moon takes 29.5 days to orbit Earth once.

From Earth, the Moon looks big and bright. But the Moon does not make its own light. It reflects

On the Moon

Twelve astronauts have walked on the Moon. The first moonwalks took place in 1969 and the last in 1972. The temperature on the Moon ranges from 250° Fahrenheit (121° C) to –250° Fahrenheit (–121° C). There is also no air to breathe. Astronauts wore spacesuits to protect themselves. They collected rocks to give to scientists on Earth.

light from the Sun. The amount of sunlight that the Moon reflects back to Earth changes. This makes the Moon look like it has a different shape every night. The different shapes are the Moon's phases.

The Moon has dark areas and light areas. The dark areas are large basins called maria. A basin is a round, shallow hole. Maria are filled with dark lava rock. The light areas are mountains of light-colored rock. Small rocks and gray, dustlike soil cover the Moon.

Thousands of craters dot the surface of the Moon. Many craters are small, but others are more than 100 miles (161 km) across.

Mars's reddish color made astronomers in early times think of blood. They named the planet after the Roman god of war.

Mars, the Red Planet

Mars is the fourth and last rocky planet. It orbits 142 million miles (228 million km) away from the Sun. Mars has a bigger orbit to travel than the other inner planets. It takes longer to circle the Sun than Earth does. One year on Mars is 687 Earth days long.

Mars is the third smallest planet in the solar system. Mars has a diameter of 4,217 miles (6,787 km). It is about half the size of Earth.

Like all planets, Mars spins on its axis. A day on Mars is 24 hours and 37 minutes long.

The atmosphere on Mars is made mostly of carbon dioxide. Martian air is 100 times thinner than Earth's air. People would not be able to breathe it.

Missions to Mars

Scientists have sent more than 30 space probes to Mars. About half the space probes failed to complete their missions. Several space probes were very successful. They sent back many pictures and a great deal of information about Mars.

The United States sent two *Viking* space probes to Mars in the 1970s. They took thousands of pictures of Mars. These pictures showed that Mars has volcanoes, canyons, dry river valleys, and craters. *Viking* landers touched down on the surface of Mars. The landers dug in the Martian dirt. They tested soil and looked for living things.

In 1997, the *Pathfinder* space probe landed on Mars. It carried a small robot car called *Sojourner*. *Sojourner* rolled over the surface of Mars studying rocks. *Pathfinder* took pictures of *Sojourner* as it did its work.

Desert and Ice

Mars is a red planet. Its surface is covered with reddish rocks, sand, and soil. The red color comes from the chemical iron oxide. Iron oxide is also called rust.

Martian wind blows dust around the planet. Strong winds create huge dust storms that can last

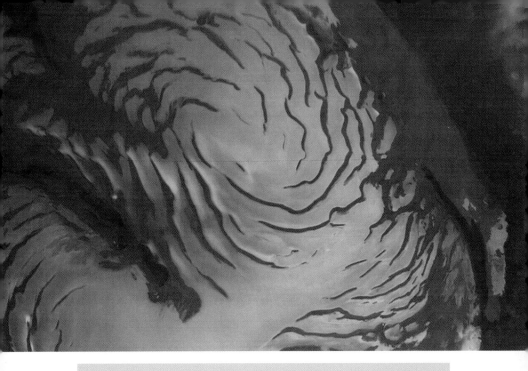

This picture shows what Mars's north polar
ice cap looks like in summer.

for months. The wind blows the dust and sand into
dunes, or hills. These dunes cover many open areas
on Mars.

Cold winters cause ice to form on Mars. Frozen
carbon-dioxide gas forms one kind of ice called dry
ice. It never melts. Carbon dioxide can either be a
gas or a solid, but not a liquid. Frozen water makes
up the second kind of ice. Dry ice and frozen water
make up ice caps surrounding the North and South
Poles on Mars.

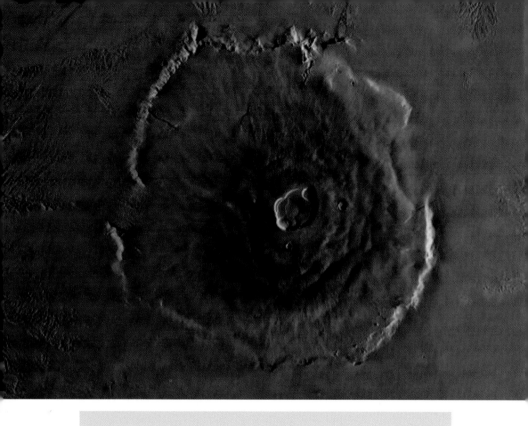

Mars's Olympus Mons volcano is the largest known volcano in the solar system.

Surface Features

Dry river channels stretch across Mars. Some astronomers think Mars had a thicker atmosphere in its past. The planet would have been warmer. Water would have flowed through the river channels. If so, the rivers might have cut the stream valleys. Some of the water may have soaked into the surface and frozen. Scientists think the rest of the water probably escaped into outer space.

Mars has many giant, inactive volcanoes. The largest volcano is Olympus Mons. It is 16 miles (25 km) high. The volcano's base is about 374 miles (550 km) wide. This is wider than the states of New Hampshire and Vermont put together. At the top of the volcano is a 50-mile (80-km) wide crater. The crater was once a lake of molten lava.

The giant Valles Marineris canyon is also on Mars. This canyon stretches about one-fifth of the way around the planet. It is about 2,500 miles (4,022 km) long. Parts of the canyon are more than 125 miles (201 km) wide. Some parts of it are 5 miles (8 km) deep. It is much bigger than the 280-mile (451-km) long Grand Canyon on Earth.

In June 2000, *Mars Global Surveyor* took new, close-up pictures of Mars. Some scientists believe these pictures prove that there may be some liquid water on Mars today. The pictures showed features that look like gullies. A gully is a long, narrow ditch. Scientists think moving water formed the gullies on Mars. They believe water from beneath Mars's surface flooded the land. They do not know what caused the flooding.

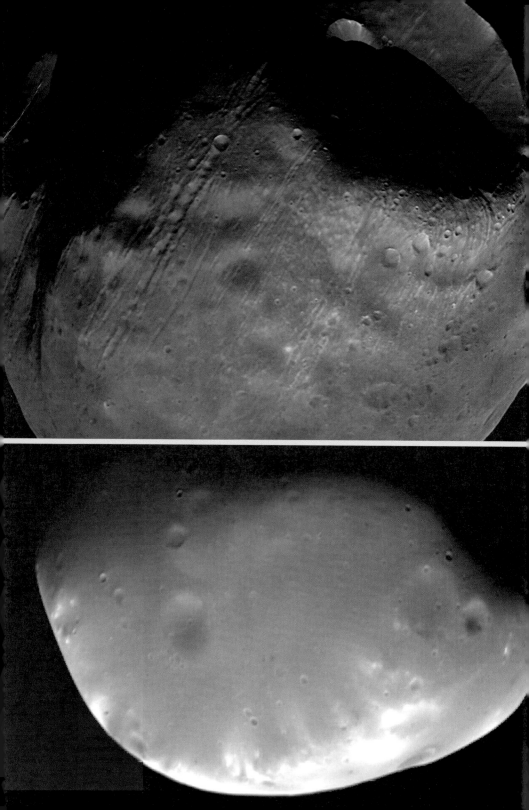

Phobos and Deimos

Two moons orbit Mars. They are called Phobos and Deimos. The moons were named after the sons of the Roman god Mars. Phobos means fear. Deimos means panic.

The moons are very small. Phobos is 17 miles (27 km) across. Deimos is 9.3 miles (15 km) across. To see the moons, people need powerful telescopes.

Phobos and Deimos are shaped like two giant potatoes. Bumps, scratches, and craters cover their surfaces. Both moons have many craters.

Phobos orbits 3,700 miles (6,000 km) above the surface of Mars. It circles the planet once every 7.6 hours. Deimos orbits 14,562 miles (23,436 km) above Mars. It circles the planet once every 30 hours.

Astronomers believe Phobos and Deimos were once asteroids. Asteroids are large rocks in space. Astronomers think the asteroids passed near Mars. Then the gravity of Mars pulled them into orbit around the planet.

Craters cover Deimos (top) and Phobos (bottom).

43

The *Sojourner* robot car rolled around Mars in 1997.

Life on Other Planets

Many people have made up stories about aliens from other planets visiting or attacking Earth. No one knows if there is life on other planets. Scientists do not know what living things on other worlds would look like.

Scientists built space probes to study the inner planets. The *Viking* landers and *Sojourner* looked for living things on Mars. So far, scientists cannot agree whether they have found signs of life on Mars or not.

Scientists are still looking for other life in the solar system. They plan to send new space probes to explore the inner planets. The space probes will take more pictures and collect more information to look for life.

Scientists also hope that they will understand Earth better by learning more about other planets. They may find out more about the forces that shape Earth and the future of our planet.

Glossary

atmosphere (AT-muhss-fihr)—a layer of gases that surrounds an object in space

crater (KRAY-tur)—a bowl-shaped hole left when a meteorite strikes an object in space

greenhouse effect (GREEN-houss uh-FEKT)—the warming of a planet's atmosphere caused by gases in the atmosphere that prevent the Sun's heat from escaping quickly into space

maria (muh-REE-ah)—round, shallow spaces full of dark, hardened lava

meteorite (MEE-tee-ur-rite)—a rock that crashes into the surface of an object in space

nebula (NEB-yoo-lah)—a huge cloud of gas and dust in space

orbit (OR-bit)—the path an object travels around another object in space

phase (FAZE)—a stage of the Moon's change in shape as it appears from Earth

rotation (roh-TAY-shuhn)—the spinning of an object in space

solar system (SOH-lur SISS-tuhm)—the Sun and all the objects that orbit it

Internet Sites and Addresses

The Moon
http://www.seds.org/billa/tnp/moon.html

NASA for Kids
http://kids.msfc.nasa.gov

Planets and Moons
http://wwwflag.wr.usgs.gov/USGSFlag/Space/wall
  /wall_txt.html

**Star Child: A Learning Center for
  Young Astronomers**
http://starchild.gsfc.nasa.gov/docs/StarChild/
  StarChild.html

NASA Headquarters
Washington, DC 20546-0001

The Planetary Society
65 North Catalina Avenue
Pasadena, CA 91106-2301

Index